Elizabeth I

WHO WAS...

Elizabeth I
The Kingly Queen

CHARLOTTE MOORE

✳ SHORT BOOKS

First published in 2005 by

Short Books

15 Highbury Terrace

London N5 1UP

10 9 8 7 6 5 4 3 2

A CIP catalogue record for this book
is available from the British Library.

ISBN 1-904977-09-X

Printed in Great Britain by
Bookmarque Ltd, Croydon, Surrey

For William, Katharine, Helena and Stella Moore

The Two Rings

" Robin, I am faint!"

The great Queen half lay, half sat, propped on a pile of cushions in the Withdrawing Chamber at her palace of Richmond. She stretched out a hand, once white and graceful, now blotched with age, gnarled like the roots of an ancient oak. Sir Robin Carey took his kinswoman's hand with tenderness and reverence. He pressed it to his lips, noticing that Elizabeth's coronation ring had grown into the flesh of her finger. Its jewels glowed rich as ever, but round it the skin was swollen and purple. Dare he say anything? Elizabeth had had this ring placed upon her finger forty-four years before, as a symbol of her bond to her people and her country, and with superstitious love she had never removed it.

He touched the ring with one fingertip, and cleared his throat. Elizabeth read his mind.

"Yes, indeed, Robin, the time has come when my ring and I must part company. Pray call for the goldsmith; I cannot loosen it; he must saw it off for me. But this one" – she indicated a second ring, a circle of gold and enamel, a man's ring. "This one, Robin, I shall keep."

Sir Robin bowed low. He did not ask the significance of this second ring, but he thought he could guess. The gift of the Earl of Essex, the handsomest, bravest, most foolhardy courtier of all who had graced the court of Gloriana, as Elizabeth's admirers had called her! Essex, whose fall from grace had been as spectacular as his rise. The Queen's last great love – and yet, in the end, put to death, when even she could no longer overlook his treachery and overweening ambition.

So, she still kept Essex's ring. Sir Robin was struck by the loneliness that comes with greatness. His eyes misted with tears.

"I will seek out a goldsmith directly, madam. And

may I also urge your Majesty to – "

"Call a doctor? Never, Robin! To what end should I preserve this crooked carcase? Though my ring be hewn from my finger, my bond of loyalty to my country may not be so lightly broken. The last service I can perform for my beloved England is to die quickly."

CHAPTER ONE
A Goodly Child

She was born on a blue and gold morning more than seventy years earlier on Sunday 7th September, 1533. "The child that is born on the Sabbath Day, /Is bonny and blithe and good and gay," the old rhyme tells us. Elizabeth could be all those things; she was many other things besides.

The royal palace at Greenwich was chosen as the best place for this special baby's birth. It was close to the River Thames, which made for easy access in those days when travelling by water was safer and quicker than travelling by road. It was in a healthy position, removed from the filth and stench of the City. And it was at Greenwich that her father, King Henry VIII, had been born, forty-two years before. She was meant to follow in her father's footsteps. She was meant to be a boy.

King Henry was desperate for a son, a prince who he could train in the art of government. He wanted an heir who was strong, clever, popular and just, able to unite the warring factions of the realm and rule over a prosperous, well-defended nation. He couldn't imagine that a mere girl could rule like that. No, it had to be a boy.

As a young man, Henry had been tall, fine-looking, with long legs and red-gold hair. He was a sportsman, a musician, a poet, equally skilled in the arts of war and peace. He was clever, generous, with a loud infectious laugh; if you were in Henry's favour, he warmed you like the sun. But he was also cruel and ruthless, and, in the end, tyrannical. If you withstood him, you risked being cast into the chill of endless night.

Now, in middle age, Henry had lost his youthful good looks. But in his presence you never doubted that he was one of the most powerful rulers in the world. He planted his long, strong legs widely apart as if to straddle the globe; a red beard fringed his fleshy face and added to the sense of bulk. His sword, his chains and his rings, his doublet of heavy embroidered brocade, his velvet breeches slashed to reveal the rich silk lining – all in all, he was an impressive, fearsome spectacle. He was a great man, and this was his baby.

Anne Boleyn was already pregnant when Henry married her on January 25th 1533. The physicians and soothsayers assured the royal couple that the baby would be a boy – well, they would, wouldn't they? The celebrations were planned weeks, even months, in advance.

Queen Anne's bedchamber was carefully prepared for the birth. Arras – that is, tapestry – woven with gold and silver threads covered the walls and ceiling. There was thick carpet on the floor. Light and air were considered dangerous for both mother and baby, so there was only one small window. In the late summer heat, Anne must have felt half suffocated. No pictures of people or animals were woven into the tapestries, in case they gave Anne imaginative fantasies which might deform the unborn child. Only simple patterns were allowed. An altar stood in the bedchamber, furnished with gold and silver crucifixes and candlesticks.

On 26th August, the Queen drank wine and spices with her courtiers, who prayed to God to "give her the good hour". Then everyone formed a procession to escort Anne to her bedchamber, where she remained alone but for her waiting-women, until the birth was over.

And the looked-for prince did not arrive. Anne was delivered of a child who was healthy, beautiful – but female. The celebratory pageant was cancelled.

No woman had ever yet ruled England as queen in her own right. There had been plenty of queens, of course, but they'd all been the wives of kings. Some were powerful, resourceful women, well able to influence their royal husband and command the respect of nobles and commoners alike. But none had ever ruled alone. The very idea was shocking.

If Henry could have seen into the future, how astonished he would have been to learn that his daughter Elizabeth became all these things and more. Elizabeth

I was the most popular and successful monarch England ever had. Her long reign was a golden age for art, poetry, the theatre, for scientific discovery, for travel and exploration. Elizabeth, the little princess whose arrival was such a bitter disappointment, became more famous and respected than Henry himself. Even today, Elizabeth's image is everywhere. We all recognise that pale oval face, that halo of red-gold hair, that stiff lace ruff, that steady dark-eyed gaze.

In the midst of her disappointment, Anne could not help noticing with satisfaction that the tiny Princess Elizabeth had her father's red-gold hair – the hair of the House of Tudor.

***

"How pretty! The purple and the white satin together – see how they set one another off! And the gold netting over all! These dainty caps will well become my little lady."

Dorcas the lady's-maid chattered as she unwrapped the latest gifts that Queen Anne had sent her little daughter. Lady Bryan, governess to Princess Elizabeth, laid down her goose-quill pen. She was glad to be diverted from the tedious work of writing out the week's housekeeping accounts. She came over to admire the little caps, running her fingertips over the embroidery so that she could relish the fine workmanship.

"There's no doubt about it, Her Majesty adores her little daughter," said Dorcas. "See how she showers her with gifts! Last week, the gold and silver trimmings for her great bed, and now these pretty caps. And the King, too – our lady Elizabeth is much in her father's favour, as such a goodly child should be."

"Dorcas, how you do rattle on!" reproved Lady Bryan. She glanced through to the adjoining chamber, where Elizabeth lay on her bed of state, taking her afternoon nap. She looked absurdly tiny, curled up in the middle of that immense bed with its carved oaken pillars and heavy damask hangings, but such grand furniture befitted her royal status. A separate household had been set up for Elizabeth when she was only three months old – in those days, royal babies were not looked after by their own parents. Little Elizabeth had lain on that great bed to receive important visitors before she could either walk or talk. But now, aged two, she could do both – and what a forward child she was turning out to be! If Lady Bryan wanted to indulge in gossip with the maid, she needed to be sure her little mistress was asleep. It was astonishing how much Elizabeth already understood of what she overheard.

"But I wonder when Her Majesty will grace us with her presence?" mused Dorcas as she stored the satin caps in muslin bags scented with lavender. " 'Tis many weeks since last she visited our household."

"Her health, perchance, was weakened by her untimely delivery," suggested Lady Bryan. Anne Boleyn's last pregnancy had come to a premature end: she had been "delivered of a foetus, of appearance male". It was said that Henry's rage and disappointment at the news had been terrifying to behold.

The King was full of guilt. And it had only added to his pains that Anne's miscarriage had occurred on the very day of the funeral of his first wife, Catherine of Aragon, Poor Catherine! Henry's burning desire for a son had led him to do desperate things. Henry and Catherine had shared many interests, and for fifteen years the marriage had worked. Henry had respected Catherine's intelligence and strong moral sense;

Catherine had been full of admiration for her talented, good-looking husband. But of the six children she had borne, five had been still-born, or else died soon after birth. The only child to survive had been little Mary. Henry could hardly believe his bad luck, to have reached the age of forty-two with only a single, sickly daughter to his credit.

And then Catherine's health had begun to fail. She had taken solace in her Catholic faith. To Henry, it seemed that she was always praying, weeping or fasting. And Mary grew up to be just as pious as her mother. The sight of the two of them, down on their knees, mumbling over their rosary beads, had made Henry feel quite sick.

No wonder his eye had been caught by young Anne, a slender girl full of energy and grace, very different from Catherine. She was no princess; she was little more than a commoner. People could not understand what Henry saw in her. She wasn't even an outstanding beauty, but her dancing dark eyes and teasing, playful ways had him spellbound. Anne's enemies – and there were many – rumoured that she was a witch.

Henry had wanted her, badly. But Anne would be no

idle plaything, for the King to dally with and then cast aside. She would be Queen, or nothing. And if she was to become Queen, Henry had to marry her.

Five hundred years ago, divorce was not the straight-forward process it is today. England was a Catholic country; the King of England was answerable to the Pope of Rome, head of the Catholic Church. To divorce Catherine, Henry had to convince the Pope to release him from his marriage.

Unsurprisingly, the Pope said no. And Henry had behaved like a spoiled child. If the Pope won't let me divorce, he said, I'm not going to accept his authority. He had broken away from the traditional Roman Catholic faith, and started the Church of England, based on Protestant teachings. To this day, the reigning British monarch is also head of the Church of England.

Cheating and bullying, or courageously cutting links with an oppressive hierarchy – whichever way you judge Henry's behaviour, it had got him what he wanted. And yet how quickly things changed...

***

Dorcas glanced about her, and lowered her voice. "They do say," she confided, "that His Majesty is not so partial to the Queen as once he was. And there is another, much in favour – my lady Jane Seymour. 'Tis said, she and the King have ridden out these several days together – "

"Hold your tongue, Dorcas! Speak no disrespect." Lady Bryan knew she should seem stern, but secretly she longed to hear more. So often, servant girls were the most reliable sources of information. And Dorcas's own sister Martha waited on the Queen herself...

Lady Bryan returned to her desk, and once more dipped her quill pen in the inkwell. But Dorcas was well used to her mistress's ways. She knew Lady Bryan's reprimand meant little, that she found it easier to listen to gossip if her back was turned. Dorcas cleared her throat.

"If 'tis true His Majesty's fancy wanders, then 'tis no great wonder if the Queen does likewise. What's sauce for the goose is sauce for the gander, say I."

The squeaky scratch of Lady Bryan's quill on parchment was her only reply, but the coiled braids pinned on either side of her head looked like a pair of listening ears.

"And the Queen's a young woman yet. She's always been... spirited. If His Majesty neglects her, there'll be others to take his place."

"At what risk to their own necks!" Lady Bryan could forbear no longer.

"What hot-blooded young man wouldn't risk his all for a fair lady's favour? Especially when – " Dorcas's giggle was nervous – "especially when that lady is versed in the magic arts!"

"Fie, Dorcas, you speak slander! Our Queen is no witch. Remember your place, my girl. Your livelihood depends upon Her Majesty – and mine does too, I'll allow. And above all, speak no ill of the most royal mother of our little Lady Elizabeth. Hold your tongue and sort the linen. There's three or four chemises are spotted with the mould for want of airing." And Lady Bryan resumed her list-making, a cold finger of fear prodding at her heart. If Anne could not produce a living son for the King, it might be that her days were numbered. And then, what would become of them all?

In the next chamber, the sun shone through the stained-glass window, dropping pools of molten colour on the counterpane – liquid sapphire, ruby and emerald.

Little Elizabeth loved to touch the colours with her finger, loved to watch her own white skin take colour. She had lain awake for a while now, just watching and listening. They spoke of her mother, she knew – the mother whose visits filled Elizabeth with warring emotions of excitement and dread. "Our Queen is no witch." So she'd heard Lady Bryan say. But Elizabeth called to mind her mother's raven hair and darting eyes, eyes so dark they were almost black. She was only two years old, but she knew about witches. And she knew that the safest thing was to lie still, say nothing, give nothing away.

***

Henry's second marriage was growing stale. His passion for Anne Boleyn had run its course; moreover, no boy child was forthcoming. Pale, solemn-faced Jane Seymour occupied an ever-greater part of the King's mind. Jane was sweet, gentle, virtuous – the opposite of the flighty and flirtatious Anne.

Henry needed Anne out of the way, so that he could marry Jane. This time, he didn't think about divorce. He accused Anne of having a string of lovers, including her own brother. We will never know if the accusations were true. But once Henry had made up his mind to get rid of Anne there was no saving her, however hotly she protested her innocence. She was tried, found guilty of adultery, and condemned to death.

Anne was locked up in the Tower of London, the traitors' jail. She met her death – execution by sword – with spirit and valour. Elizabeth was two years and eight months old. We don't know whether she remembered her mother. Her whole life long, Elizabeth never wrote or spoke a single word about Anne Boleyn.

Was she silent because she wanted to rid her mind of the horror of her mother's terrible fate? Or was it a canny political decision, to associate herself in the eyes of other people with Henry, her powerful parent, and hope they'd forget her connection with poor disgraced Anne?

As soon as her mother was branded a whore, Elizabeth's life took a turn for the worse. Like her half-sister Mary, Elizabeth was treated as a "bastard". The supply of pretty gifts dried up. Now, Elizabeth had scarcely enough clothes to keep her warm. Lady Bryan wrote letters begging for more supplies. It wasn't easy bringing up a royal child when her father the King provided so little money

***

"Well, little sister, so we are to rejoice." Mary Tudor, seventeen years older than Elizabeth, had never been the easiest of sisters. Her emotions blew hot and cold. Sometimes she fawned upon the child, praising her prettiness, her intelligence, her piety. Sometime she hugged her and shed tears, wallowing in sympathy, calling Elizabeth her sister in misfortune, the two of them blighted by the shadow of their father's disfavour. And sometimes Mary showed jealousy, almost hatred, and taunted Elizabeth as the bastard child of Anne, the hated usurper, the sloe-eyed witch who had ruined the life of Mary's own saintly mother. When Mary was in this mood, Elizabeth had learned to give her a wide berth.

But now they had a half-brother. King Henry's new bride had provided him with the longed-for son. Good, gentle Jane Seymour had died in childbirth, and that was unfortunate, but Henry had his little Prince Edward.

The future of the House of Tudor rested on those infant shoulders. Henry was so delighted with his son that he could afford to soften his attitude towards his daughters.

Mary sat down close to Elizabeth on the oak settle by the fireplace. With one hand, she caressed the head of a sad-eyed mastiff who rested his vast head upon her knee. Elizabeth noticed how small and thin her sister's hand looked, like a bird's claw. She noticed, too, the black mourning ring that Mary always wore, in memory of her mother.

Mary held her face close to Elizabeth's. Her teeth were crooked and blackened, her breath sour. Elizabeth tried not to flinch. It took all her self-control to put up with having her sister this close. Poor Mary was short, plain and sickly. Her unhappiness and her many illnesses had destroyed her looks. Her skin was rough and pitted, her hair and eyes dull. Elizabeth could not help thinking that Mary's dark red velvet gown only made her skin look yellower.

"Rejoice, sister? What is the cause?"

"Have you not heard, Elizabeth? Parliament has passed the Act. Our places in the succession are assured. If our brother Edward should die childless – as I pray

Heaven will not allow – first I, then you, may follow him to the throne, and our children after us. If by God's grace, it should fall to my lot so to do, I will strive with all my might to restore and revive the one true church, and so would you too, my sister, I do heartily believe."

Mary tried to fix her sister with a look of sharp enquiry, but Elizabeth kept her eyes cast down. She did not want to be forced by Mary into a firm commitment to either the Catholic or the new Protestant church. Young as she was, she would play a political game with her religion, hinting to Mary that she was a devout Catholic, while assuring her father of her loyalty to his own creation, the Protestant Church of England.

Mary clasped Elizabeth's hand in her own. She held it uncomfortably tight. "Pray, little sister! Pray to God to give you guidance!" she hissed. To Elizabeth's relief, the schoolroom bell range, summoning her to her lessons. She pulled free of Mary's embrace and withdrew, honouring her with a low curtsy. Her most fervent prayer to God at that moment was that He make her sister's stay a short one.

Poor Mary! She had plenty of reasons to be jealous. As Elizabeth skipped off to the schoolroom she looked every inch a princess. Tall for her age, slender, with exquisite, long-fingered hands, a graceful neck, milky skin, and hair that gleamed like copper... her forehead was high, her nose long but shapely, her mouth narrow (as was then admired), her eyes clear and questioning. This was a face beyond mere prettiness. It expressed high intelligence, and a wisdom beyond her years.

Mary had no extraordinary talents to mark her out. Her most striking characteristics were her religious fervour and her limitless capacity for bitterness. She was intelligent enough, but in comparison with Elizabeth... Elizabeth was something else.

People flatter princes and princesses, and exaggerate their talents. There can be no doubt, though, that Elizabeth was a gifted child. The sixteenth century was a golden age for the education of women – of high-born women, that is. Henry wanted his daughter to be the best educated girl in Europe. Scholars from Cambridge University were employed to teach her to the highest level. At the age of nine, her mornings were spent studying Ancient Greek. In the afternoons she worked at Latin, French, Spanish and Italian. Throughout her life, Elizabeth prided herself on her languages. When she was over sixty, she amazed the court by rebuking the Polish ambassador in fluent Latin. The first time she saw Shakespeare's play *Love's Labours Lost*, she translated it into Italian as it went along, for the benefit of an Italian guest of honour who didn' t know English.

The young Elizabeth also spent hours on her handwriting. Her tutor, Roger Ascham, taught her the beautiful but complicated italic script, from which she developed her famous swirling signature. This handwriting looked decorative, but it had another purpose too. In the sixteenth century, spies and forgers were everywhere. Complicated unfakeable handwriting was an asset for an important person like Elizabeth.

Elizabeth also studied religion. England was still reeling under the shock of Henry's break with the Pope; arguments between Protestants and Catholics raged. Elizabeth's brother Edward was passionately interested in religious questions from an early age. He loved to discuss such matters with his sister, in person and by letter.

This was a heavy timetable for the young princess. But her scholarship was balanced by other activities. She loved riding. She was an excellent dancer. She was musical, like her father; when she played the virginals, an early keyboard instrument, it gave her a chance to display her dainty white fingers as well as her musical talent.

But no part of Elizabeth's life was really free from worry and danger. The middle part of her childhood was probably the happiest. She felt safer then than at most other stages of her life. But her early experience of treachery, bereavement and the fickleness of royal favour left her wary and suspicious, good at keeping secrets and protecting herself.

***

When she was thirteen and a half, everything changed. The centre of her world – the centre, to some people, of the entire world – was thrown off balance. Her father, feared and beloved, admired and detested – the great King Henry VIII was dead.

The event was expected, yet unthinkable, unimaginable. Henry's health had been bad for some time. He had become bloated, obese. His cruel, greedy eyes could hardly squint out of his puffed blackened face. His swollen legs were covered with running sores, which smelled terrible. He could no longer support his own immense weight; a special winch-lift was built, to haul him from one place to another, and he was carried about on a litter. His temper was as foul as his breath. It was obvious that he could not live long. And yet so great was his power, so dominant his personality, that the news of his death still came as a terrible shock. He had acted as though he could live for ever, and no one had dared tell him otherwise.

Prince Edward was only nine years old when Henry died. He became King Edward VI, but was too young to rule in his own right. So Henry had left him under the control of Edward Seymour, brother of Edward's dead mother Jane. How would Elizabeth fare now that the radiance of her father's capricious goodwill had been forever extinguished?

CHAPTER TWO

Sickly Edward and Bloody Mary

"Kat, Kat, help me!"

The squeals came from behind the clipped box hedges in the sunlit garden. The box trees smelled warm in the sun, a musty, tom-cat smell. Mistress Kat Ashley, governess to the Princess Elizabeth, paused in her picking of the flat pink roses with the curled golden stamens at their scented hearts which her young mistress loved to float in glass dishes to perfume her bed chamber. What was going on?

"My lord, my lord, for shame!"

Was Elizabeth in jest or in earnest? Her shrill cries were joined by a deep, mocking man's voice, a voice

Mistress Ashley knew very well. She could not suppress a smile. The Lord Seymour! New husband to Katherine Parr, the widow of King Henry, and therefore stepfather, in a sense, to Princess Elizabeth. A man with a ready wit, a charming smile; a proper man! He was a tease, that was for sure; Elizabeth's squeals suggested he was up to his tricks again. And now there was another voice, a woman's.

"Hold still, child. See how this new fashion becomes you! There – and there – and there!" It was the voice of Katherine Parr herself, warm and humorous. Elizabeth was in no danger. But what could they be up to? Kat laid her basket on the grass, and peeped round the corner of the hedge.

Elizabeth, tall for her thirteen years, halfway between child and woman, stood at the centre of the parterre. Her hands were over her face – was she laughing or in tears? Katherine, so recently a dignified queen of England, had her arms clasped round Elizabeth's waist; face flushed, she giggled like a young girl. And what was Thomas Seymour doing? This great nobleman, brother to the Lord Protector of England… was he really cutting his stepdaughter's white muslin gown into ribbons? The silver scissors flashed in the sunlight; he raised them again and again. "There, Lizzie, we'll make a proper mammet of you! Where's my haughty princess now?"

Elizabeth uncovered her face, and caught sight of Mistress Ashley. "Oh Kat, dear Kat, save me from these torturers!" She was weak with laughter, but there was a note of panic in her voice as well. As Kat stepped forward, Seymour raised the scissors once more. "The gown is done. Now for the hair!"

Elizabeth screamed. Her hands would have flown to protect her tight-coiled braids, but Katherine Parr restrained her. Mistress Ashley couldn't bear it. That beautiful, copper-coloured Tudor hair! She rushed forward. "My lord, my lord, forbear!"

Thomas Seymour laid down the scissors. "Why, Kat," he grinned, "do you not trust me? This was a jest, I swear. Do you think I would cut one single hair, one of these golden threads that are her crowning glory?" He aimed a playful pat at Kat's broad rump. Katherine released the trembling Elizabeth. Seymour took the princess by the shoulders and twirled her round so that the shreds of her dress flew up like the ribbons of a maypole.

"There, little girl, run along and play. We have sported enough for one day." Seymour took his wife's arm; laughing, they strolled back to the house.

Kat Ashley looked into her young charge's face, but couldn't read what she saw there. Elizabeth's face was as pale as usual, but her cheeks glowed as pink as the flat roses, and her eyes were bright. "Oh Kat, 'twas all in sport," she whispered. Kat's gaze turned to the receding

figure of Lord Seymour. All in sport – maybe so, but what did this sporting mean?

***

Katherine Parr had been Henry VIII's sixth and last wife – the only one to avoid divorce or death. She was warm-hearted and intelligent; she had made a fine job of managing her foul-tempered husband during his final illness. She had persuaded him to acknowledge both Mary and Elizabeth as his legitimate daughters and restore them to the rank of princesses instead of just "ladies". And after Henry's death she tried to provide the three orphans with some sense of family and love. She was especially close to Elizabeth, and invited her to share her home in Chelsea.

Elizabeth admired her stepmother. She had watched Katherine acting as Henry's deputy when he was abroad, and the experience showed her that a woman could make political decisions and give orders to men.

Katherine had had no intention of remaining a widow for long. When Henry died, she had been still quite young and lively, and had been delighted when

Thomas Seymour started wooing her. Thomas could charm the birds out of the trees; whatever affection he felt for Katherine Parr, his ambition was a stronger drive. And, once married to Katherine, Thomas had grown closer and closer to the teenage princess.

What did Thomas mean, when he cut Elizabeth's dress to ribbons, or when he climbed into her bed in the morning and tickled her until she was helpless with laughter? Was he just a playful stepfather whose idea of fun sometimes went a little too far? Or was he flirting with Elizabeth, to turn her into his puppet, his plaything, to help pave his way to political power? Already, Elizabeth was the darling of the English people. Of Henry's three children, she was the most like her father, and whatever Henry's faults, he'd always been a popular king. In the game of political success, having Elizabeth on his side had to be a good thing for Thomas Seymour.

While Katherine Parr lived, the attraction between Thomas and Elizabeth remained as a kind of teasing game, but in September 1548 Katherine died giving birth to a daughter. Now the game became serious. Would Thomas marry Elizabeth, young as she was? Elizabeth's governess, Kat Ashley, held her breath. She thought Thomas was marvellous and had sung his praises to Elizabeth day and night.

Thomas Seymour had always been a reckless, ambitious man. His brother, the Lord Protector, didn't trust him – that was common knowledge. Was Thomas plotting to usurp his brother's power? Was he even plotting to do away with frail young Edward and put Elizabeth on the throne instead? Thomas had been protected by his wife's high status as King Henry's widow, but after her death, his behaviour grew wilder.

Protector Somerset couldn't risk it. His brother Thomas was too dangerous to remain alive. So Thomas was charged with thirty-three counts of high treason, and locked in the Tower. The bile rose in Kat Ashley's throat when she heard the news of his execution. Such a goodly man! So warm, so vibrant, so alive! And now, his handsome head sliced from his body by the cruel axe!

***

The first portrait we have of Elizabeth alone was painted at about this time. She stands poised between childhood and womanhood. Beneath her pearl edged crimson dress with its wide heavy sleeves we see the living, breathing lines of a growing body. Her oval face is calm, almost mask-like, but her dark, wide-spaced eyes are knowing. She holds our gaze. Elizabeth is wise beyond her years. We see a real girl, but a girl who has already learned to distance herself from trouble.

Before he died, Thomas Seymour stitched a farewell note to Elizabeth into the sole of his velvet shoe. When Elizabeth heard the news of his death, she remarked, "This day died a man of much wit and very little judgement." She had been half in love, but she had not allowed her heart to rule her head. The feelings she suppressed can only be guessed at. But for the rest of her life, all the men she ever loved bore a marked resemblance to the doomed Thomas Seymour.

***

King Edward had been a vigorous child. He was a good scholar; he also enjoyed hunting and taking part in mock tournaments. But in 1552 he caught measles and smallpox. The following year, the first dreaded signs of tuberculosis (TB) showed themselves. TB, also called consumption, is a disease which attacks the lungs. Until penicillin was discovered in the twentieth century there was no effective medical treatment for it. By May 1553 it was obvious that Edward hadn't long to live.

"The sputum which he brings up is livid, black, fetid and full of carbon; it smells beyond measure," reported his doctor. Edward, a fanatical Protestant, was tormented with anxiety about his Catholic sister Mary becoming queen, but he faced his death bravely. On 6th July, he murmured, "I am faint: Lord have mercy on me and take my soul." These were the last words he spoke.

Mary was on her way to London to visit her brother when she heard that he had died, and that the Duke of Northumberland (who had succeeded Edward Seymour as Lord Protector) had proclaimed his young daughter-in-law Lady Jane Grey as queen of England. Mary rallied her supporters; it was clear that most people agreed that she was the lawful queen, and on 19th July the Lord Mayor of London proclaimed her as such. Northumberland was arrested. Lady Jane Grey, pitiful queen for nine days, was carted off to the Tower.

Clad in royal purple and gold, Mary rode in triumph

to London. There she met Elizabeth who was decked out in the Tudor livery colours of green and white. The two sisters embraced with joy.

But before long, Mary was putting pressure on Elizabeth to convert to the Catholic faith – the one true faith, as Mary saw it. During her five-year reign, Mary's main aim as queen was to restore the Catholic church in England and to wipe out Protestantism, regardless of how much blood was shed.

***

Mary was desperate to marry. In the sixteenth century, people married earlier than they do now. Mary was thirty-seven; many would have been grandmothers by that age, but Mary was still single. Now she was Queen, she could choose her own husband. She chose Philip of Spain, who was eleven years younger. This was a deeply unpopular choice. Philip was a foreigner, and a Catholic! The Spanish Embassy in London was pelted with snowballs in protest.

But Mary was stubborn, like a true Tudor. She had set her heart on Philip. Not only would he help her in her fight against the Protestants, but it just so happened that she'd fallen in love with him. Mary's heart, shrivelled by years of loneliness and grievance, swelled and blossomed when Philip was near. She leaned on him, looked up to him, let him do whatever he liked.

Early in 1554, Sir Thomas Wyatt led a rebellion against Mary, Philip and Catholicism. The rebels marched from Kent to London in an attempt to push Mary off the throne and put Elizabeth in her place. Mary made a brave and rousing speech, urging Londoners to fight back. The uprising was quelled, and Wyatt and his supporters put to death. Elizabeth protested that she had known nothing about Wyatt's plot, but Mary didn't believe her, and ordered her to leave her country home for London where she could be closely watched.

Elizabeth pleaded illness. Mary forced her to make the journey anyway. Elizabeth, dressed in white, the colour of innocence, travelled in an uncovered litter, to show the people that she was not afraid or ashamed. As usual, she won all hearts and minds. Ordinary people, peasants and villagers, loaded her litter with gifts of cakes and flowers as she passed by.

London had become a city of horror and desolation. The heads of executed traitors were left to rot on spikes for all to see. Bodies of hanged men dangled from the gallows in awful warning. Poor sweet Lady Jane Grey, the innocent victim of her father-in-law's ambitions, had had to watch the headless body of her beloved young husband Guildford Dudley being brought back from the scaffold; soon afterwards, she was herself beheaded.

In vain, Elizabeth protested that she was a loyal sister. She begged to be allowed to see Mary, but Mary refused, fearing, perhaps, that at the sight of Elizabeth kneeling at her feet her heart would melt. Elizabeth wrote a letter, the most important letter of her life so far. "I pray God as evil persuasions persuade not one sister against the other," she wrote. "I humbly crave but only one word of answer from yourself."

No answer came. Mary ordered Elizabeth to be taken by barge to the Tower. As she was led towards the river, Elizabeth looked up at the windows of the Queen's lodging, hoping to catch sight of Mary. But no face looked out.

The barge carried Elizabeth down the Thames from Whitehall to the Tower, landing at the Traitors' Stairs.

Next, she had to walk past cages of roaring lions, past the block where Lady Jane Grey had laid her blindfolded head. Elizabeth looked up to heaven and declared to the warders and soldiers, "I never thought to have come in here as prisoner; and I pray you all, good friends and fellows, bear me witness that I come in no traitor but as true a woman to the Queen's majesty as any is now living: and thereon will I take my death."

One of her fellow-prisoners in the Tower meant a lot to Elizabeth. Robert Dudley, son of the recently executed Duke of Northumberland, was exactly the same age as Elizabeth – his date of birth is uncertain, but legend has it that they were born at the same hour on the same day. In childhood they had been companions, and had shared a tutor, Roger Ascham. Their relationship had become deeper and deeper over the years; indeed Robert came to know Elizabeth better than anyone else on earth. We can't be sure whether they were able to make contact with one another during their imprisonment. But it is tempting to believe the story that the warder's little boy smuggled messages between the two friends, including a robin's egg – a code for Robert Dudley's nickname, Robin – hidden in a posy of flowers. Another story tells us that Elizabeth scratched these words on a pane of glass with her diamond ring:

> *Much suspected by [= of] me,*
> *Nothing proved can be,*
> *Quoth Elizabeth, prisoner.*

Mary had enough sense to see that her subjects

wouldn't tolerate the death or ill-treatment of their beloved Princess Elizabeth. The people flocked in their thousands to hear an echo known as the "spirit in the wall". When they cried "God save Queen Mary!" the echo was silent, but when the cry changed to "God save the Lady Elizabeth!" the echo replied "So be it!"

At last, Mary had to admit that there was no proof of Elizabeth's guilt, and released her. Her hour of greatest danger had passed. Mary's mind was occupied with two things – destroying Protestantism, and trying to have a baby. She became known as "Bloody Mary" because she put so many Protestants to death, often by burning them alive. As for babies, she was obsessed by her desire for them, to pass her crown on to a good Catholic child of her own, to keep herself in favour with her husband Philip, who soon showed signs of losing interest in her, and – perhaps above all – to fulfil her yearning for someone to love.

Mary's stomach swelled, and her breasts produced milk; overjoyed, she retreated to her bedchamber, fully convinced she was about to give birth. But no baby appeared. After three months, Mary re-emerged, mortified; the doctors could not account for this "phantom pregnancy." The same thing happened again. So strong was Mary's belief in her pregnancy that the birth of a son was announced, to public rejoicing. But that son never existed. Watching her sister go through all this may have strengthened Elizabeth's private resolve never to try for babies herself.

Mary, sallow, often doubled up in pain, an old woman before her time, was at last forced to accept that her younger, prettier, popular, Protestant sister would inherit the throne. Philip spent most of his time abroad; he was now Mary's husband in name only. Mary became sicker by the day. On November 17th 1558, she died. On her deathbed, she believed that she was surrounded by little children, singing and playing like angels.

Elizabeth had said that she would not believe her sister had died until she saw her black and gold engagement ring. She knew that Mary, living, would never part from this. On the day Mary died, Elizabeth was at Hatfield House in Hertfordshire, walking in the park in the chill November mists. She looked up to see messengers on horseback, breathless, flecked with sweat. They had galloped from London with the news. Among them was Sir Nicholas Throckmorton, a courtier and diplomat. From inside his jerkin he produced Mary's ring.

Elizabeth touched it, then knelt on the cold grass beneath a spreading oak tree, the symbol of England. "This is the Lord's doing; it is marvellous in our eyes" – these were the first words she spoke as Queen. She was quoting the Bible, which would please the Protestants, but she quoted it in Latin, which would please the Catholics. Her ability to balance the warring factions was typical of the way she ruled throughout her long, supremely successful reign.

CHAPTER THREE

Men, Marriage, and Mary, Queen of Scots

England breathed a sigh of relief. Sour-faced, diseased, fanatical Queen Mary was gone. The hangings, the tortures, the burnings, belonged to the past. Her hated husband Philip had gone back to Spain. In place of Philip and Mary was Elizabeth, slender, graceful, full of wit and laughter, crowned with the red-gold Tudor hair, just like her father's. The whole nation was jubilant.

The new Queen rode in procession to the Tower of London, resplendent in purple velvet. How very different was this from her last entrance there, as Mary's prisoner! The nobles and commoners alike swore their love and loyalty to her. Nosegays were pressed into her hands every step of the way. Elizabeth had the common touch. Throughout her reign, she had a knack of turning her royal processions into conversations. At once grand and approachable, these "progresses" were her way of keeping in contact with her people.

The royal astrologer John Dee consulted the stars, and chose 15th January 1559 as an especially lucky day for the coronation. Elizabeth crossed London in an open litter draped with gold brocade. By her side marched gentlemen pensioners in crimson damask carrying gilt battle-axes, and footmen in crimson and silver velvet jerkins decorated with the Tudor rose. The city streets ran with wine. Along the way, pageants were performed, with actors in fancy dress reciting verses about Elizabeth's life so far and the nation's hopes for the future.

Elizabeth was crowned in Westminster Abbey in accordance with ancient and sacred rituals. The noise of organs, fifes, trumpets, bells, drums, and the happy shouts of the crowd made it seem, said one observer, as if the world had come to an end. Her magnificent coronation robes cost £16,000.

But for all the goodwill her people bore her, there

were rumblings of doubt. The royal household numbered fifteen hundred people, most of them men. How could this young woman hope to control them? Unlike her father, she couldn't make them fear her; grown men don't tremble at the command of a mere girl. Elizabeth knew she had to rely on character and intelligence. An elaborate courtly game arose, an artificial comedy in which the men all vowed they were in love with her, and competed as to who could pay her the wittiest compliments or come up with the most eye-catching gifts. Elizabeth danced and flirted and accepted endless presents of jewels and perfumes and embroidered gloves. It was all a game, but it was a game with a purpose – to build up power and control over her courtiers.

Some of the lords hardly bothered to take in Elizabeth's talents and qualities, because they assumed she would soon marry. Then her husband would be king, and of course he would have all the real power. No one expected Elizabeth to stay single for long. How could any of them have guessed that save for those who, like Edward VI, died very young, Elizabeth would be the only English monarch to die unwed?

Was this her own choice, or did the right man never

come along at the right time? Robert Dudley, who saw further into her mind than most, said that when she was only seven years old she had decided never to marry. And by the time she was grown up she had seen plenty to put her off. Her own mother for a start – Henry had risked everything to marry her, but then she'd had her pretty neck sliced through by the executioner's sword. Henry's next wife, Jane Seymour, had died in childbirth, as had Katherine Parr, of whom Elizabeth had been so fond. Silly, pretty Catherine Howard, the fifth of Henry's six wives, had also had her head cut off when she ceased to please his majesty. And then Elizabeth had watched her sister Mary sicken and debase herself for love of Philip, who used any excuse to get away from her. No, marriage was a risky business, in Elizabeth's experience.

But if Elizabeth died childless, the royal House of Tudor would come to an end. Every loyal subject hoped, prayed, expected, that Elizabeth would give birth to a child who would rule after her.

Elizabeth was the most eligible woman in Europe, and she knew it. Every royal family on the continent put forward a prince or an archduke as a possible husband for her. But marrying a foreigner was a problem in itself.

You won the friendship, riches and support of one country, but your husband's enemies became your enemies too. And most of the foreign princes were Catholics. Elizabeth, a Protestant herself, didn't want to upset her supporters by marrying a Catholic. Look how the English people had hated Philip of Spain!

It was easier to find a Protestant husband amongst the English aristocracy. But then, Elizabeth would be marrying beneath her. By definition, no man in England was the equal of the Queen. A husband, in those days was supposed to give his wife orders. How could a Queen take orders from anyone?

Elizabeth's choice of husband – or of no husband – was a fascinating topic of discussion for people in the sixteenth century, just as the love-lives of film stars and famous singers are talked about today. And it was much more important, because the Queen's decision affected everybody's lives. Elizabeth knew how to use her celebrity mystique to powerful effect. For years, she kept everyone guessing. She played off one suitor against another, scooping up their gifts and compliments as she did so. Would she choose Eric, Prince of Sweden? She accepted his ambassador's generous presents, but laughed at his outlandish ways. Or what about one of the sons of the Austrian Emperor? And Philip II of Spain himself saw no problem in the idea of marrying his dead wife's younger and far more attractive sister. Later, Catherine de Medici, powerful matriarch of the French royal family, was very pushy in her attempts to interest Elizabeth in her many sons.

Elizabeth had trained herself to hide her true emotions. She knew she could never marry for love alone. But she scorned to marry a man for whom she could feel no affection or respect, whatever his wealth, power or noble birth. And all this time a flame burned in her heart for Robert Dudley, whom she had known all her life. Perhaps her feelings for him helped her to resist the temptation to choose any of the other suitors.

When Elizabeth came to the throne, aged twenty-five, she had outlived mother, father, brother and sister. She was very much alone. No wonder she clung to familiar people, to her old governess Kat Ashley, to her chief minister William Cecil who was like a father to her, and above all to Robert Dudley.

As soon as she became queen, Elizabeth made Robert her Master of the Horse. He rode back to London with her, on that first triumphant day of her new reign. They made a fine sight, the straight-backed, flame-haired young queen, and her beloved "Robin", with his russet curls and neat, pointed beard, laughing and joking by her side.

Robert was a married man, but it was easy to forget that. At seventeen, he had married a young heiress, Amy Robsart. William Cecil remarked that this marriage, having "begun in passion, ended in mourning". There were no children, and soon the couple were leading separate lives. This suited Elizabeth. She could see her "Eyes", as she nicknamed Robert, as much as she wanted, but she could not be suspected of planning to marry him.

But two years after Elizabeth became queen, poor lonely Amy was found dead at the bottom of the stairs in the country house she so rarely shared with Robert. In her misery, had she thrown herself to her death? Or – some tongues were not slow to whisper – had she been pushed? Had Robert paid an assassin to get rid of her, so that he could marry Elizabeth and become King of England?

It's equally possible that Amy's death was an accident. She was ill, probably with cancer; she may well have stumbled and tripped. And it didn't make Elizabeth more likely to marry Robert – the opposite, in fact. Elizabeth needed to distance herself from the whole sad business. She couldn't bear anyone to suspect that she had had a hand in Amy's death. This queen, unlike many of her predecessors, did not believe in having people quickly killed just to suit her own convenience.

***

Unless Elizabeth had a child, her heir would be her cousin, Mary, Queen of Scots – a fact which made William Cecil and her other advisors even more anxious for her to marry.

Mary was a foreigner. She had been born in Scotland, which at that time was completely independent from England. Her father James V had died when she was only six days old, which made her Queen of Scotland. But when she was four, she had been sent to live at the French court, as the intended bride of François, the Dauphin, or crown prince, of France. As one Englishman put it, this left "the French king bestriding the realm, having one foot in Calais and the other in Scotland".

So the Queen of Scots was the second important Mary in Elizabeth's life. She could hardly have been more different from dour, plain, vengeful Mary Tudor! The cousins were fated never to meet, but they were fascinated by each other, and wrote to one another often. They had plenty in common. Both were young women of strong character, slim and attractive. Both were good dancers and expert horsewomen, both loved poetry and music, and both were intelligent, though Mary was not as scholarly as Elizabeth. Mary had been brought up in the French way; French was her first language, and she had elegant, courtly manners. She was exceptionally tall – nearly six foot, in those days when any woman who reached five foot four was regarded as tall – and was considered a great beauty.

But there were crucial differences, too. Elizabeth was cautious, restrained; she kept her strong feelings under control. She was a shrewd judge of character, and she surrounded herself with people she could trust. Mary, on the other hand, was a hot-headed romantic, governed by powerful emotions. She was headstrong and stubborn

– so was Elizabeth, but unlike Mary she could listen to reason. John Knox, a fiery Scottish preacher who was bitterly opposed to Mary, said that she had "a proud mind, a crafty wit, and an indurate heart". And, fatally, Mary had the habit of falling in love with desperately unsuitable men.

As soon as she was old enough, Mary married François, and when he succeeded to the throne, she became Queen of France. But he soon died of a brain tumour; Mary nursed him tenderly, and shut herself in her room to mourn him for forty days. She was a widow at the age of only eighteen. Now was the time for her to return to Scotland and take up the reins as queen. Would Cousin Elizabeth grant her a safeguard, so that she could make the difficult and dangerous journey with protection against bandits and brigands, and against any who might be plotting against her life?

Elizabeth paced the long gallery, Mary's letter in her hand. Mary had spent almost all her life in France, while Elizabeth had never set foot abroad. But now, with Mary returning to Scotland, they would be closer neighbours. Should she offer protection to this cousin she had never met?

Her first instinct was to help. Mary was not only her cousin and sister-queen, but she was young, vulnerable, recently bereaved. Elizabeth's heart went out to her. But this generous impulse was checked by caution. How far was Mary to be trusted, being a Catholic and heir to the English throne? And besides, all those who had seen Mary raved about her beauty, her charm, her vivacity, her talents. Mary was taller than Elizabeth, younger, and possessed of the fatal ability to make people fall in love with her. Elizabeth stood at the mullioned window. She breathed a mist onto the glass, then traced a question mark with her forefinger.

A heavy footfall interrupted her reverie. Her heart lifted. She'd know that slow, deliberate tread anywhere! It was William Cecil, her chief adviser, the man whose opinion she valued above all others, the man who sometimes seemed to think her thoughts for her – her "Spirit", as she nicknamed him. She turned to greet him. Cecil was reassuringly solid, his hair and beard already threaded with grey. He was dressed as always in long, black, fur-trimmed robes, black cap, and chain of office made of thick golden links. His lined and pendulous face lit up at the sight of his young sovereign.

"My Spirit!" She took his broad, be-ringed hands between her slender ones. "I have need of your counsel. What think you of this letter, just arrived from my cousin of Scotland and of France?" To spare Cecil's embarrassment, Elizabeth read the letter aloud, translating as she did so. Mary had written in French, and Cecil's knowledge of languages was rudimentary compared to her own.

Cecil frowned as she read. He had an instinctive distrust of all foreigners, especially Catholic ones. The news that Mary was to return to Scotland was most unwelcome. Any Catholics who wanted to get Elizabeth off her throne would want to put Mary in her place. Cecil pulled at his long beard, deep in thought.

"Your Majesty will smile," he said at last, "because I recommend caution, and as you will say, when did Cecil ever advise otherwise? But let us not forget that the Queen of Scots did in pride and insolence display the arms of England upon her own coat-of-arms. The father of her late husband never ceased to claim that Mary was rightful Queen of England, and it seems that Mary holds that same wrong-headed belief herself, whatever her protestations of loyalty to Your Highness." Cecil was wise enough not to mention that Mary's claim to the throne of England rested on the idea that the marriage of Anne Boleyn and Henry VIII had not been lawful, and that Elizabeth was therefore illegitimate. Cecil knew that any mention of her parents' marriage made Elizabeth's hackles rise.

"So, Sir Spirit, guide me. Shall I help my cousin to pass in safety through this land? Or should I let her feel the edge of my displeasure?"

"Do neither, madam. Delay is your ally. Grant her no safeguard, but neither provoke her to any wrath. Do not be too hasty to pen your letter of reply."

Mary made the journey anyway, by ship instead of by land. She arrived in Edinburgh to a heroine's welcome. The Scots were delighted to have their young queen back. They fired cannons in salute, and played music beneath her chamber window, though to her French-educated ears their instruments sounded less melodious than the roar of the cannons.

But the rejoicing was short-lived. Many Scots were strongly opposed to a Catholic ruler. As with Elizabeth, there was the question of who Mary should marry. Elizabeth, like many of the Scottish nobles, did not want

Mary to marry a second foreign prince, so giving another foreign country a foothold in the British Isles. To avoid this, Elizabeth even offered Robert Dudley, her beloved "Eyes", as a suitable husband for Mary. She quickly made him Earl of Leicester to make the match a more equal one; during the ennoblement ceremony, she teasingly tickled his neck with her ceremonial sword. But Mary refused.

Elizabeth buried her negative feelings about Mary. She wrote to her offering support, and several times she tried to arrange a meeting between them, but each time something happened to prevent it – bad weather, bad health, a political crisis.

In the end, Mary answered the marriage question herself, in the worst possible way. She chose her cousin, Henry, Lord Darnley, who was only eighteen, blond, "beardless and lady-faced". Mary fell head-over-heels in love with this amusing, lively youth; she said he was "the lustiest and best-proportioned long man that she had ever seen", and indeed his height was a big part of the attraction. It was hard for the exceptionally tall Mary to find a man who she could literally look up to.

On the three nights before Darnley's arrival in Edinburgh for the wedding, the shouts and clashing weapons of ghostly warriors could be heard on the streets at midnight. But Mary chose to ignore these bad omens, just as she chose to overlook the truth about her new husband's character. He was debauched, drunken, dishonest, and mentally unstable.

Darnley became great friends with David Rizzio, Mary's Italian secretary, who was a gifted musician. Darnley and Rizzio were party animals who loved to go out carousing together. But Darnley's friendship for Rizzio soon turned to jealous hatred. Mary and Rizzio were close – too close. She said she loved to hear him play music for her – what else did she love him to do? When Mary became pregnant, Darnley believed that the baby was Rizzio's, not his own.

One evening, when Rizzio was at supper with Mary, Darnley and his accomplices burst in, dragged Rizzio out of the room, and struck him down with daggers. There were fifty-six stab wounds on his body. "Woe the time," wrote the English ambassador to Scotland, "that ever the Lord Darnley set his foot in this country! What shall become of her, or what life with him she shall lead... I leave it to others to think!"

Mary was six months pregnant at the time of Rizzio's murder. She shed bitter tears, as well she might. In marrying for love, she had made many enemies. Now that love was turned to sour hate, and her beloved secretary was a mangled corpse. Though Mary had many faults, cowardice was not one of them. She dried her eyes. "No more tears. I will think upon a revenge!"

Elizabeth supported Mary at this difficult time. She was moved, in particular, by a letter Mary sent her, dictated in Scottish dialect rather than written in her usual French. Mary said that she was too exhausted to write the letter herself: "Bot of trewt we ar so tyrit & weill at eass, quhat throw rydding of twenty millis in v horis of the night... in the grittest danger feir of our lyvis that evir princes on earth stuid in." ["But in truth I am so tired and ill at ease, what with riding twenty miles in the hours of night... in the greatest danger and fear of my life that any princess on earth was ever in."]

Elizabeth described the horrors of Mary's plight to

her courtiers in forceful terms. She took to hanging a miniature portrait of Mary from her waist by a gold chain. If she herself had witnessed Rizzio's death, she declared, she would have taken Darnley's dagger and stabbed him with it. And when Mary's son James was born, on 19th June 1566, she gladly agreed to be his god-mother, and sent a massive golden font as a christening present.

And yet Elizabeth, now thirty-three, must also have felt a pang of envy at the news. The story goes that she was dancing when a messenger arrived to tell of little James's birth; and she stopped dancing, to exclaim: "The Queen of Scots is lighter of a fair son, but I am but a barren stock!"

It wasn't long before foolish, brave, passionate Mary was in love again. Once more, her choice was a disaster. James Bothwell was described as a "vainglorious, rash and hazardous young man". Mary thought he was strong, that he would protect her from her enemies and help her rule this wild land of Scotland. But James was mad for power and excitement, and would stop at noth-ing. And soon he had got Mary into deep trouble, with the two of them suspected of murder...

The story goes that Darnley had fallen ill, and Mary had lured him to a house outside Edinburgh city walls, promising that he would be well nursed there, and giving him a ring in pledge of her love. She had then departed at night, by torchlight. It is true that both Bothwell and Mary wanted dreadful Darnley out of their way. But it is also possible that Mary's motives were innocent. For, whatever she felt about Bothwell, she was not necessarily planning to marry him at this stage. And she may well have wanted to mend her marriage, for the sake of baby James.

Either way, at two in the morning, the house where Darnley was staying was ripped apart by an explosion. Darnley's dead body was found next day in the garden. But it was not the explosion that killed him. He had been strangled.

Edinburgh was aflame with excitement about the grisly crime. Many people suspected that James Bothwell had masterminded the murder, but there were other suspects, too – Darnley had plenty of enemies. Mary, unwisely, responded by showering favours upon Bothwell, and declared that for his sake she'd go to the world's end in a white petticoat.

On April 24th, 1567, when little James was only ten months old, Mary, though she did not know it, kissed him goodbye for the last time. She rode from Stirling to Edinburgh, and was waylaid by Bothwell, who carried her off to Dunbar. Some said he forced her into marriage against her will, others that she was his willing accomplice. Whatever the truth, they were quickly married by a Protestant ceremony. Once again, what Mary thought was true love turned into something monstrous. Only two days after this, her third wedding, Mary was calling for a knife with which to kill herself.

Now the Queen of Scots had few supporters left. Her marriage to Bothwell was hugely unpopular. The pair of them were attacked by their enemies. Bothwell escaped, but Mary, who was again pregnant, bravely struggled on until she was taken captive and brought back to Edinburgh. Just six years earlier the citizens had welcomed her warmly. Now they shouted, "Burn the murderess!"

Mary was imprisoned in a fortress on the isle of Lochleven. Here her pregnancy ended miserably – she miscarried twins. Bothwell escaped to Norway and was never to see Mary again.

The Scottish lords told Mary to abdicate her throne in favour of her baby son. Heavy with sorrow, she agreed. And so little James became King James VI of Scotland, with his uncle the Earl of Moray as regent.

Elizabeth did not like this outcome. She still wanted Mary to be queen, though she had wanted her rid of Bothwell. When Mary escaped from her island prison, Elizabeth wrote congratulating her in her own hand.

Mary raised a troop of supporters, but they were defeated by the Earl of Moray's army. She then fled to England across the Solway Firth with nothing save the clothes she stood up in. Here was a new problem for Elizabeth. What should she do with her cousin, once her equal as reigning queen, now a pitiful fugitive? She wanted to bring Mary to court and honour her, but her councillors persuaded her that this would be unwise.

So, for the next eighteen years, Mary was kept in captivity in a succession of English castles and country houses. Elizabeth paid £52 a week of her own money – a great deal in those days – to make sure that Mary was comfortable and well treated. But this was not enough for the passionate Mary, who was soon embroiled in Catholic plots to remove Elizabeth from her throne. The problem of what to do with her tempestuous cousin would remain a thorn in Elizabeth's side for a large part of her reign.

CHAPTER FOUR
Gloriana

There had never been a monarch as popular as Elizabeth. Even her father, "Bluff King Hal", or "Great Harry", as he was known, had not been quite so revered and adored. Poets celebrated their queen as "Gloriana"; she was worshipped almost like a goddess.

Vain though she was, Elizabeth did not let the flattery go to her head. She was always aware that she was no goddess but a mere mortal with her share of faults and weaknesses. But she played on her popularity; she knew that no one could rule effectively if they didn' t inspire loyalty, love and awe in their people. She worked hard to live up to the image of "Gloriana", in the public mind at least.

One way of maintaining this image was to pay stately visits to her noblemen in their great houses. Whether these visits lasted for weeks or for only a few days, Elizabeth and her train had to be royally entertained. And her aristocratic hosts competed with each other as to who could put on the best show in her honour.

One such visit was made to the Earl of Hertford at Elvetham. Elizabeth only stayed for three days, but three hundred men were set to work to enlarge the house, build extra housing for the royal servants, and dig a giant pond in the shape of a crescent moon. In the pond were three islands, one shaped like a ship, the second like a fort, and the third like a snail. When the Queen arrived, she was greeted by a poet wearing green to signify his joyful thoughts; while he recited his Latin poem, six virgins strewed the path with flowers and sang a sweet song in six parts.

The next day Elizabeth watched a display on the great pond. Nereus, the prophet of the sea, swam ahead of five Tritons – sea-gods with multicoloured hair and beards – blowing their horns. Then came the gods Neptune and Oceanus drawing a boat containing sea-nymphs, who carried jewels to present to the Queen.

When Elizabeth looked out of her window in the morning, three musicians broke into song. That evening, a magnificent firework display took place on the three islands. While the Queen and her courtiers watched, they were served a banquet by two hundred gentlemen. There were more than a thousand dishes, all glass or silver.

On her last morning, Elizabeth was saluted by the Fairy Queen and her maids. When she came to depart, they sang a song called "Come Again," which ended,

"O come again, sweet beauty's sun:
When thou art gone, our joys are done."

I wonder how sincere the Earl of Hertford was in asking the Queen to "come again"; her visit had cost him a small fortune.

Elizabeth was quite well aware of the expenses she incurred with these visits. And it pleased her, as it meant that she didn't have to pay for the upkeep of her court all the time – she was always looking for ways to economise without cutting back on her royal grandeur. At the same time, by forcing her hosts to spend lots of money on her, she was making sure they didn't get too powerful. She like to keep everyone and everything under control.

Nor was it only the aristocrats who paid tribute to "Gloriana". Wherever she went, she was showered with presents by her loyal people. At Coventry, for example, the Mayor presented her with a silver cup containing £100 in gold coins. "But, Your Majesty," he explained, "it contains a great deal more than that."

Elizabeth asked him to explain. "It also contains the hearts of all your loving subjects," he said.

"We thank you, Mr Mayor," replied Elizabeth, "That is a great deal more, indeed."

And, though her noblemen and supporters might pull long faces at the sight of the enormous bills she incurred, the situation also undoubtedly suited them. In the case of the Earl of Hertford, for example, it was due to Elizabeth, in a sense, that he was able even to consider putting on such a display. In the past, in more warlike times, noblemen had had to spend their fortunes on training and equipping soldiers; you never knew when your private army might be called into your country's service. But Elizabeth had brought peace and prosperity to her troubled land. She was a good housekeeper; she hated war because it was a waste of money as well as a waste of human life.

As a result, noblemen like the Earl of Hertford had the money and the leisure to spend on their homes and gardens. In Elizabeth's time, the country houses belonging to the "great" families became less like fortresses and more like pleasure palaces. Rich men bought beautifully carved furniture, intricately woven tapestries, and paintings by skilled artists, including the fashionable miniature paintings, which were exquisitely detailed and often encased in jewelled, enamelled frames. They had their gardens laid out in complicated designs, often with symbolic meanings. Their clothes, too, became richer and more elaborate. It took at least two servants to help an Elizabethan gentleman to dress. They wore lace cuffs and ruffs, padded detachable sleeves, long stockings, puffed velvet knickerbockers and tight, embroidered doublets. They often carried swords, but these were more for ornament than for use. All the money that was spent on these things was money that, under a more bloodthirsty sovereign, would have been taken away in taxes to pay for foreign wars.

When Elizabeth became queen, England had been a country on the brink of ruin. Plague had rampaged through many towns and villages. War against France had been costly and unsuccessful. The enmity between Protestants and Catholics was fierce and bitter.

Elizabeth had seen that what the country needed most was stability. She always tried to solve problems through diplomacy first; bloodshed was a last resort. And with religious disputes, too, she sought the middle way. She was reluctant to force men's consciences – and equally reluctant to make martyrs of those who opposed her.

Elizabeth's golden rule was to do the opposite of whatever her sister Mary would have done. When she came to the throne she made two promises to the English people. One was that she would always take advice, always listen to her counsellors. The other was that she would never lose the love of her people, never provoke them to rebellion. She saw herself as a mother to the people of England, and as a wife to England itself.

Elizabeth surrounded herself with wise counsellors whom she could trust. She was very loyal to her advisers, and they in turn served her with devotion. Chief among them, of course, was William Cecil later Lord Burghley. He helped her with all her political decisions until his death, nearly forty years after she became queen. When he lay dying, Elizabeth fed him with her own hands. After his death, her eyes would fill with tears whenever his name was mentioned.

Elizabeth gave nicknames to all her favourite people. Cecil was her "Spirit", Sir Christopher Hatton "Lids" or "Mutton", Sir Walter Raleigh was "Water", Archbishop Whitgift her "Black Husband". Robert Cecil, William's tiny, humpbacked son, was "Pygmy", which he didn't care for much, or "Elf", which was slightly better. This affectionate teasing helped to strengthen the bonds of loyalty.

Like her father, Elizabeth knew how to put on a good show. She presented herself as a kind of approachable goddess. She knew that her physical appearance had to be grand and impressive – queenly, in fact. During her brother Edward's reign, Elizabeth hadn't worn particularly rich jewels and fine clothes. She had conveyed the impression of a modest young girl, shaming the other court ladies who were "dressed and painted like peacocks". But once she became queen, such modesty was no longer appropriate.

Elizabeth was a vain woman. She was proud of her Tudor red hair, her pale skin, her elegant hands. But she also knew that she could make a greater impact if she emphasised, even exaggerated, her trademark features. She was a politician through and through; even the way she looked was a political decision.

When her own hair became thin and grey, she wore high-piled orange wigs that framed her oval face and provided nests for her clusters of jewels. In old age the effect was almost grotesque, but at least it was memorable. In those days a tanned skin was a sign of low status, because it suggested that you worked outside in the fields to earn your living. The paler your skin, the bluer your veins, the higher your social status. Obsessed with preserving her famous milky-white complexion, Elizabeth had a special face-cream made to a secret recipe based on ground almonds. As she grew older, she used thick white make-up, too, to almost clown-like effect.

Elizabeth adored perfumes and cosmetics. In those days of poor drainage when bad smells were everywhere, rich people often carried something sweet-smelling to sniff. She was always delighted by presents of lace, jewellery, fans, and embroidered stockings and gloves. When she died, she left behind three hundred dresses – at that time even a fairly rich woman would have had only six, and a poor woman would be lucky to have more than one.

Elizabeth's dresses were so stiff with embroidery and precious stones that they could stand up by themselves. But her clothes did more than simply reflect her love of finery. They gave her a distinctive image, an image which became famous throughout the world.

Elizabeth's dresses had tight-fitting bodices, long, detachable sleeves with delicate lace at the wrists, and wide skirts, often stretched over a stiff frame called a farthingale. Sometimes the skirts were looped back to reveal patterned petticoats underneath. The skirts reached to the ground; in those days, the only part of the body on display was the neck and upper part of the chest. The legs could only be glimpsed during dances. Elizabeth made the most of her long, elegant neck by wearing stiff lace ruffs that whirled and curled as intricately as her handwriting.

Wearing a farthingale made her already narrow waist

look even tinier, and the bulk and width of her skirts meant that she could only move in a stately, careful manner, as befitted a queen. Beneath the hem of her dress, her little feet peeped out, encased in satin shoes as heavily ornamented as everything else she wore. These clothes were designed for display, not for comfort or strenuous activity. Of course Elizabeth had other costumes, less grand, more practical, for riding, walking, and other activities, but these were not the clothes she wore when she sat for her many portraits.

Elizabeth had learned how important portraits were from her father. In paintings of Henry VIII, he plants his legs far apart and looks at the viewer full on; he dominates the picture as he dominated his court. Henry's portraits spell power and strength; they helped to spread his fearsome reputation throughout Europe.

Elizabeth's portraits became even more celebrated. To this day, her pale, oval face framed with its ruff is recognised everywhere. In those days before photography, looking at a portrait was the only way you could know what your queen looked like, unless you were lucky enough to catch a glimpse of her on one of her royal progresses. Elizabeth made sure that copies of her portraits were hung in town halls and great houses the length and breadth of the land. Pubs and inns called "The Queen's Head" proudly displayed her image on their wooden signs. These pictures did not exactly reflect what Elizabeth really looked like. Rather, they were reflections of the way she *wanted* people to see her.

For official appearances, Elizabeth favoured gowns that were either pure white or black. Both made a strong impact. She also liked purple or violet, because it was a royal colour, and because it made a memorable contrast with her red-gold hair. Pearls were her favourite ornament; in her portraits she is often hung with ropes and ropes of them.

Elizabeth and her court were always on the move. She would spend a month or two at each of her palaces, moving from Greenwich to Whitehall to Richmond to Hampton Court to Windsor and back again. In the days before proper sanitation, this was a good idea. All the dirt and mess made by the Queen and her retinue of courtiers and servants could be thoroughly disposed of after her departure. And besides, in those days almost all food had to be provided by local suppliers. There were no fridges or freezers to keep food fresh, no aeroplanes, trains or lorries to carry food quickly from one place to another. The Queen and her courtiers descended like a swarm of locusts and ate everything in sight. When food stocks ran low, it was time to move on.

The Elizabethan court took eating seriously. Two vast meals a day would be served, one at eleven a.m., one at five p.m. Every meal was a banquet, but on feast days, such as Christmas, Twelfth Night and Easter, the food was even more elaborate, the table decorations extra ingenious, the diners' costumes more fanciful than ever. At the Christmas feast, a "great pie" was the centre-piece, a huge pastry "coffin" into which were crammed meats of every kind, beef, mutton, capons, mallards, rabbits, hares, woodcock and teal. These were mixed with egg yolks, dates, raisins and prunes, and flavoured with cloves, mace, cinnamon and saffron. In those days before refrigeration, spices were very important both in helping to preserve meat, and for disguising the taste of meat that had already begun to go off. Venison was a very popular meat, often served with a peppery sauce or roasted in spiced wine. Roast peacocks were impressive, laid out on platters decorated with their own magnificent blue and green tail feathers.

Meat and fish of all kinds would be followed by jellies, candies made of pine nuts and honey, and marchpane (a sweetmeat like hard marzipan) fashioned into the shape of ships, coats-of-arms and heraldic beasts. While the courtiers ate, they would be entertained by plays, ballets, musicians, even bull- and bear-baiting, though these bloodthirsty sports would probably not whet appetites nowadays! The performers were rewarded with titbits from the table, sweetmeats, cheese, nuts and spiced wine.

From the descriptions of the feasting, you might imagine that the Elizabethan courtiers were all hugely fat, but this was not so. For one thing, exercise was fashionable; led by the Queen's example, both men and women took part in vigorous dancing, walking, riding and hunting. And though the banqueting tables were strewn with dozens of different dishes, most people only took a couple of mouthfuls of each. The plenty was there for show. And the feasts were not as wasteful as they seemed. At the end of each meal, alms baskets were filled with leftovers to be distributed amongst the poor.

The Queen herself was more a spectator than a

consumer at these feasts. She had a small appetite, and preferred to eat simple meals in private. But she did have a weakness for sugary treats. As a result, her teeth became rotten. By the end of her life most of them had been pulled out and replaced with false ones.

All in all, Elizabeth's reign is remembered as a golden age for England. She encouraged artists, scientists, explorers and writers to produce their best work. She loved music, drama and poetry. One of the greatest poets of her time was Edmund Spenser, who wrote his famous poem *The Faerie Queen* in her honour. Even more important was William Shakespeare, who, to this day, is considered the

greatest English writer who ever lived. Elizabeth often invited Shakespeare and his company of actors to perform his plays especially for her.

Elizabeth never travelled abroad. She never even visited the far north or west of her own country; in those days, there was no method of transport that was faster than a galloping horse, and Elizabeth wouldn't risk being too far from London in case her enemies tried to seize power while she was away. But she loved to hear traveller's tales. She gave encouragement and rich rewards to adventurous sailors like Sir Francis Drake, the first Englishman to sail round the world. The Spaniards had discovered gold in South America. They sent cargo ships to bring the treasure back to Spain, and of course they wanted it all to themselves. So they tried to prevent ships from other countries from sailing the "Spanish Main", as they called the South Atlantic ocean. But Sir Francis Drake knew no fear. He attacked Spanish ships, seized their booty and brought it home for his queen.

To some, Drake seems little more than a pirate. But Elizabeth was delighted with the treasure he plundered. She always needed more money, and Drake and the other explorers were very important to her.

When he returned from his trip round the world, she came to greet him on his ship, *The Golden Hind*. She bade him kneel, drew a sword, and told him she was going to cut off his head. Of course she did no such thing, but knighted him instead.

Gold, silver and jewels were not all that mattered to her. Other explorers, like Sir Walter Raleigh, tried to establish English settlements in the "New World", as North America was then called.

It was a vast, unexplored land, full of dangers. The first English settlers were attacked by the native Indians or defeated by disease or the unfamiliar climate. But they paved the way for the settlers who came after them. The State of Virginia was named by Raleigh in hon-

our of Elizabeth, the Virgin Queen. The exploits of Raleigh and his followers laid the foundations of the British Empire, the largest Empire the world has ever known.

Chapter Five
"God Blew, And They Were Scattered"

Above all else, Elizabeth wanted to keep her people united. And she knew that religion was the issue most likely to tear them apart. Elizabeth was proud to be Protestant, and was not too bothered when the Pope decided to "excommunicate" her. But though she strengthened Protestant power in England, she tried to do so without resorting to bloodshed. Those who refused to go to Protestant services were not tortured; they were fined twelve pence.

Of course, there were still many Catholics who wanted to get rid of Elizabeth and replace her with Mary, Queen of Scots. Mary had been kept a prisoner in England ever since her disastrous flight from Scotland at the age of twenty-four. Many monarchs would have got rid of someone as troublesome as Mary. It would have been easy enough to have her secretly murdered. Mary's health wasn't good; no one would have been surprised if she'd been found dead in her bed one morning. But Elizabeth would not do this.

Mary spent her days praying, tending her pet birds and lapdogs. She was a talented seamstress, and sent many examples of her needlework as presents to Elizabeth. These innocent pastimes were a thin disguise for more sinister activities, for when she wasn't sewing or praying or playing with animals, Mary was plotting – plotting with the Catholics to overthrow her cousin.

Although, to Elizabeth, Mary presented herself as a convert to the Protestant faith, secretly she remained a good Catholic and wrote regularly to the Spanish Ambassador, to Philip II of Spain, and to the Pope. For despite her guards, Mary managed to smuggle letters out of the various houses in which she was held captive. Sometimes the letters were hidden in bottles, beer barrels or items of clothing. Sometimes they were written in code.

Mary, who had always been so attractive to men,

still tried to use her feminine appeal to get them to do what she wanted. She planned to marry the Duke of Norfolk, the foremost of England's Catholic aristocrats. The pair never met, but conducted their courtship by letter. Together with the Earls of Northumberland and Westmorland and Leonard Dacre, all powerful Catholics from the North of England, Norfolk thought he would have enough strength to topple Elizabeth and rule as King of England with his wife Mary by his side.

But Mary's secret letters were not as secret as she supposed. Elizabeth knew at least some of what Mary was up to. She had a secret service, headed by Francis Walsingham, a very clever man always on the lookout for conspiracies and plots. Many of the letters to and from Mary were found and decoded. Elizabeth was suspicious of the Duke of Norfolk. She gave him the chance to confess all, before it went too far. He denied everything.

"What! Should I seek to marry her, being so wicked a woman, so notorious an adulteress and murderer? I love to sleep upon a safe pillow."

Elizabeth was not convinced. She challenged Norfolk on his allegiance to deal no further in the matter. But

Norfolk still didn't stop plotting. In the north, an army of Catholic rebels was mustered. Church bells were rung backwards to raise the country. The rebels entered Durham Cathedral, tore up the Bible and cast down the communion table. Catholic trappings – altars and holy water stoups – were retrieved from dunghills and other hiding places. Then the rebels marched south, but by the time they reached York they lost heart, and scattered back to their northern homes.

This rebellion was soon followed by another plot against the Queen, the Ridolfi plot. It was unmasked by William Cecil. Elizabeth couldn't overlook the Duke of Norfolk's involvement any longer. Reluctantly, she had him charged with treason. He was executed; it was the first political beheading in England for ten years. Indeed the scaffold had rotted away with disuse, so a new one had to be made for the purpose.

Now both the House of Lords and the House of Commons wanted Mary attainted with treason, but, as usual, Elizabeth was merciful. She could not stand the thought of Mary being executed. Whatever her crimes, she was still a cousin, a woman, and a sister queen.

Meanwhile, up in Scotland, Mary's son James was

growing up. No longer the baby king, he was now "an old young man", unhandsome, ungainly, "loud of voice and weak of body". But he was clever and well-educated, and he was learning to make his own decisions as king. Poor Mary clung on to the idea that she would one day be reunited with her loving son. But she hadn't seen James since he was ten months old. James cared less about his mother than about keeping in favour with Elizabeth. He was not going to go out of his way to help Mary.

Mary started writing secret letters again, this time to Anthony Babington, a Catholic who wanted to murder Elizabeth and restore Catholicism in England through a foreign invasion. Little did she know that her letters were all read by Walsingham and his spies.

This was a plot too far. Babington and two of his fellow conspirators were partially hanged, then cut down and disembowelled and cut into quarters while still alive. The executioners claimed they were acting on the Queen's orders, but Elizabeth was horrified when she heard too late of these tortures. She ordered that the next batch of conspirators should die from hanging alone, a quicker and more merciful death.

Mary was charged with treason and tried at Fotheringay Castle. Elizabeth still wanted to pardon her, but both Houses of Parliament said this would be madness. As long as Mary remained alive, she would stir up trouble. She had to die.

Mary spent the last night of her life on her knees in prayer. The next day, she kept everyone waiting for three hours. She wore a black velvet dress with a white linen veil, an outer bodice of crimson velvet, purple inner sleeves, and sky-blue stockings embroidered with silver thread and held up by green silk garters. She carried a crucifix of ivory in one hand and a Latin prayer book in the other. She was determined to meet her death in style.

She was forty-four years old, heavy, round-shouldered, puffy faced. No one could have guessed she was once a great beauty. But she met her death with courage. To her executioner she said, "I forgive you with all my heart, for now, I hope, you shall make an end of all my troubles." She removed her black dress to reveal, to everyone's astonishment, an underdress the colour of dried blood, the colour of martyrs.

It took three blows of the axe to sever Mary's head. When the executioner grasped her head to show the onlookers, it rolled away, and he was left with an auburn wig in his hand. Mary's own hair had become scant and grey. One of her little dogs, a Skye terrier, had hidden in her petticoat. Now, it crept out, and lay between her severed head and her shoulders, whimpering in a pool of its mistress's blood.

There was feasting and merrymaking in celebration of Mary's death, but Elizabeth could neither eat nor sleep. Weeping, she declared that she had never meant to sign the death warrant. She couldn't bear the fact that a fellow queen had died a traitor's death.

James was now the obvious heir, and it looked as though he would settle down and rule as a Protestant, especially once he married the Protestant Princess Anne of Denmark. The Catholic cause lost some of its menace; the idea of religion toleration and peaceful co-existence grew stronger.

***

"She is only a woman, only mistress of half an island, and yet she makes herself feared by Spain, by France, by the Empire, by all." So said Pope Sixtus V. And indeed, the time was fast approaching when Elizabeth's England would be firmly established as one of the most powerful players on the world's stage.

Philip of Spain was increasingly angry at the way the English sailors waylaid his ships and seized their cargoes. Naturally, the Spanish sailors did the same thing in return whenever they got the chance, but in the game of seizures, England was the winner. The failure of the Babington Plot alarmed Philip still more. He saw that, with Mary's death, the chances of restoring a Catholic ruler to England were shrinking. The time was ripe for an all-out war between Spain and England.

Sir Francis Drake and another talented sailor called Sir John Hawkins were in charge of the Queen's ships. They believed that attack was the best form of defence.

In April 1587 Drake entered the Spanish port of Cadiz and burned 10,000 tons of shipping. He called this "Singeing the King of Spain's beard". He then seized Cape St Vincent to prevent the Spanish fleet from assembling at Lisbon, and off the Azores he captured a rich carrack. The Admiral of the Spanish Armada set off in pursuit, but Drake gave his pursuers the slip. The Spaniards called him "El Draque" – the Dragon. They believed him to be the Devil's son. It was said he had a magic mirror which would show him Spanish ships, wherever they were in the world. It was also believed that he could control the winds and make them do his bidding.

In 1588, Philip decided to send his Armada to attack England. He prayed two or three hours daily for its success. He was sure he'd win – the Armada was much bigger than the English fleet, and Spain was richer and more powerful than England. But it had been prophesied that, for England, 1588 would be a year of wonders, and the prophecy came true.

On July 19th, messengers hurried to Elizabeth with news that the Armada had been sighted off the Lizard, the southern tip of Cornwall. When Drake heard the news, he was playing bowls at Plymouth Hoe. He didn't panic.

"We have time to finish the game and beat the Spaniards too," he calmly remarked. But the English ships got out of harbour quickly. Though the Spanish ships were bigger, the English had superior sailing qualities and better crews. They gave the Spaniards no chance to grapple and board them.

The two fleets fought a running battle up the English Channel. And on the 27th the injured Armada anchored off Calais. Drake used a surprise tactic. He filled some old ships with oil and tar, set them alight, and sent them, unmanned, to where the Spanish ships were anchored close together.

The Spaniards were terrified by the blazing ships and tried to escape. But it was dark; some ships collided, others ran aground. Some got out to sea and sailed northwards, but the English went on attacking them until they had run out of ammunition.

Then the weather changed and a great storm blew up from the south-west. The Armada – what was left of it – couldn't go back the way it had come. It tried to return to Spain by sailing round the north of Scotland. But many ships were wrecked on the rocky coasts, driven there by strong winds. In the end, less than half of the

famous Armada limped home to Spain. Only one hundred English sailors had died, and not a single English ship had been lost.

The English victory was a miracle. The country was delirious with joy. Everyone believed that God was on the English side – He had sent the winds which had scattered the enemy fleet. Never had Elizabeth been more popular.

On August 9th, mounted on a stately steed, gorgeously dressed in purple and cloth-of-gold, Elizabeth reviewed some of her special troops at Tilbury in Essex. "She passed like an Amazonian Empress through all her army," observed one onlooker. She watched a mock battle put on for her entertainment, and then, holding a truncheon as a symbol of her authority, she addressed the soldiers:

"I am come amongst you, as you see, at this time, not for my recreation and disport, but being resolved, in the midst and heat of the battle, to live or die amongst you all, to lay down for my God, and for my kingdom, and for my people, my honour and my blood, even in the dust. I know I have the body of a weak and feeble woman; but I have the heart and stomach of a King, and of a King of England, too; and I think foul scorn that Spain, or any Prince of Europe, should dare to invade the borders of my realms."

The defeat of the Spanish Armada was one of the greatest triumphs in English history. Commemorative medals were struck; a magnificent portrait was painted, showing Elizabeth in her finest jewels, her right hand placed upon a globe to symbolise her mastery of the world, while in her left she holds a fan of glowing coloured feathers. Behind her can be seen on one side the sending of the fire ships to terrify the Spanish fleet, on the other the remains of the Armada wrecked on the Scottish rocks.

And yet, amid all the rejoicing, Elizabeth was wracked with private grief. Only a month after the victory, her friend Robert Dudley was struck dead by a fever, probably malaria. The soulmate of her childhood, the man who she had loved above all others – "Sweet Robin" – was gone. Her "Eyes" had closed for ever, and Elizabeth was left to face old age alone. She took the note he had most recently sent her, and on it she wrote, HIS LAST LETTER. Then she folded it, locked it safe in her casket, and kept it by her bedside until the day of her own death.

Chapter Six

"Sweet England's Pride is Gone"

Robert Dudley's death left Elizabeth alone in her hour of glory. But she did not choose to let the world see how vulnerable she felt. She was in her mid-fifties at the time of the Armada, but she looked and behaved as if she was years younger. She enjoyed dancing six or seven galliards a morning; she still rode, still hunted. In 1592, when she was fifty-nine, a foreign traveller commented that "She need not indeed, to judge both from her person and appearance, yield much to a young girl of sixteen."

The cult of "Gloriana", of Elizabeth-worship, was still going strong. But Elizabeth knew that she was not the immortal goddess her loyal followers and portrait-painters made her out to be. Her generation was dying off – Sir Christopher Hatton, Sir Francis Walsingham... the people she had trusted and relied on – were going, and she had to get used to a whole new set.

Elizabeth's lonely heart ached for companionship. She soon found someone to soothe the pain – or so she thought. Robert Devereaux, the young Earl of Essex, was tall, charming, and very good-looking in the style Elizabeth had always favoured. Like Thomas Seymour and Robert Dudley before him, he had luxuriant curls, a chestnut beard and fine eyes. He was a courageous soldier and an outstanding sportsman. To many young men of his day, he was the ultimate hero. When Elizabeth made her famous speech at Tilbury, her attention was caught by Essex parading a company wearing the Devereaux colours of tangerine and white. He was her Master of the Horse, the position Dudley had held all those years ago.

Like the older Robert, Essex was attractive and intelligent. But both Roberts made enemies as easily as friends. Essex was the stormier character, impetuous and daring. Robert Dudley had been canny, with a strong instinct for self preservation. Essex took risks, not least in the way he treated Elizabeth. He pushed her further than anyone else dared, asking her for favours, for money, for promotion, teasing her or sulking if she denied him anything. She was in thrall to his youth and energy, and at first she nearly always gave way.

Much though Elizabeth hated wars, she had promised to send troops to help the French king Henri IV fight the Spanish. Essex, thirsty for adventure, begged her to allow him to lead this army. He went on his knees before her, arguing and pleading for two hours at a stretch. Elizabeth was reluctant to let him go, partly because she enjoyed his company at court, but she also knew that her new favourite, for all his glittering qualities, was hot-headed and unreliable, not the best person to command her troops.

At last she gave in. Essex set off to help Henri IV at the siege of Rouen. As Elizabeth had feared, Essex played at war as if it was a glorious sport. He certainly thought a lot of himself. He was preceded by six page-boys in orange velvet embroidered with gold, and he and his horse were draped in the same material, strewn with jewels. Behind him followed six trumpeters. Henri and the French nobles challenged the English to a friendly "leaping match", and Essex "did overleap them all".

In this way Essex wasted time and money, and achieved little of real importance. Elizabeth, furious, ordered him home. Essex's grief was so great that his sobs made his buttons burst off his doublet. And still he was overstepping boundaries. He knighted twenty-four of his followers, though it was the Queen's right, not his, to bestow such honours.

William Cecil was worried by Elizabeth's affection for Essex. He saw how Essex persuaded Elizabeth to give important jobs to himself and his friends; the more of Essex's gang were in power, the more pressure Essex was able to put on the Queen. Cecil was an old man; he knew he hadn't long to go. His only hope that his son, yet another Robert, whom he had trained up himself, would take over his role as Chief Secretary – the equivalent of Prime Minister.

Robert Cecil was the exact opposite of Robert, Earl of Essex. Cecil had been dropped by his nurse when he was a baby, and it was believed that this was why he was tiny, with a humpback. He was too weak to participate in most sports. But what he lacked physically, he made up for mentally. Trained as a lawyer, he was shrewd, calculating, and a clever diplomat. Essex saw Cecil as his main rival for power at court.

And certainly, a strong hand was needed at court. Though Elizabeth's England was a powerful and prosperous nation, there were still problems. 1596 was a year of bad harvests, hunger and plague. Drake and Hawkins both died in the same year, of a sickness that swept through the fleet. Elizabeth badly needed the money her piratical heroes used to bring home. Keen as ever to fill his purse, Essex led the fleet to the Azores in an attempt to capture Spanish treasure ships, but he made a stupid mistake, and the Spanish ships slipped safely into port.

Full of bombast and bluster, Essex now argued for a full-on war with Spain; the Cecils argued for peace. In addition, a rebellion was brewing in Ireland, which was then under English control. Elizabeth and Essex had a blazing row about who should be appointed to deal with this crisis. Essex insulted the Queen; Elizabeth boxed his ears "and bade him get gone and be hanged." His friends urged him to apologise, but Essex was too proud, saying he would not be Elizabeth's slave. "What! Cannot princes err? Cannot subjects receive wrong? Is an earthly power or authority infinite?"

In the midst of this quarrel, old Cecil, Lord Burghley, died at seventy-eight – a remarkable age for those times. He had faithfully served his Queen through thick and thin. And all he wanted was to go on serving her after death: "I hope to be in heaven a servitor for her and God's church." In Spain, Philip II lay dying. All at once, Elizabeth lost her greatest adviser and her greatest enemy, too, leaving her alone at the centre of the stage.

Elizabeth could not be angry with Essex for long. She was still entranced by him. When he fell ill, she sent her own doctor to tend him, and Essex sent her a sweet and humble letter of thanks. When he recovered, he was allowed to return to court, but he had not learned his lesson, and quickly fell back into his old, proud ways.

Meanwhile, the situation in Ireland had become serious. Hugh O' Neil, the wild Earl of Tyrone, had rebelled against English rule. Alone, he was not powerful enough to defeat the English, but there was a danger that Spain would send help, because Ireland was a Catholic nation.

No Englishman wanted to lead an army to defeat Tyrone. Ireland was seen as a barbaric country with a terrible climate, inhabited by savages. There was none of the glamour of leading an expedition to France. Young pages in orange velvet wouldn't get far in the Irish bogs.

At last, Essex agreed to go. Flocks of well-wishers gathered to see him off, but on the eve of departure there was a sudden storm, an evil omen. Essex arrived in Dublin in April 1599, but instead of directly attacking Ulster, he frittered away time, money, men and horses in trivial campaigns in Munster and Athlone. When at last he marched on Ulster in August, his army was sadly depleted. He had a secret meeting with Tyrone, and made a truce with him, against Elizabeth's instructions. But eavesdroppers were at work, and they reported this meeting to the Queen.

Finally, Elizabeth began to take charge – though Essex seemed irrepressible. When she ordered him to stop knighting his followers; he made thirty-eight more. She commanded him not to return from Ireland without her permission, but he did just that. He prepared a company to land in Wales, march on London and destroy "his enemies". Did he mean Elizabeth herself?

***

104

One morning in late September, Elizabeth sat at her dressing-table in her chamber at Nonesuch Palace. On her command, the leaded casement window had been opened to let in the soft, moist air of early autumn. Elizabeth loved this time of year, loved to see the white mists rolling off the river and the sun glinting on the rows of dewdrops that hung on the gossamer lines the spiders had flung from one leaf-tip to another with quick and careless grace. She loved the heavy-burdened fruit trees; the round-bellied quinces and medlars, the velvety mulberries that dropped to the path below, sticky and dark as gouts of blood. But for all the beauty of her gardens and orchards, she felt sadness in the air. The freshness and hope of spring and summer was over. This September loveliness was touched with decay.

The light breeze from the casement touched her bare arms and shoulders and made her shiver. She sat before her looking-glasses in only her petticoat and under-bodice. By her side stood her waiting-women, patient and silent until she could make up her mind what gorgeous costume she should wear that day. The whole dressing process could take hours – Her Majesty was becoming more of a ditherer as she grew older – but the ladies knew better than to interfere.

Elizabeth caught sight of her reflection and frowned. Her own hair, cut short, was nothing but a few grey wisps – where had all that copper glory gone? On a stand in front of her stood one of her many wigs, richly red, already bedecked with its freight of jewels. Elizabeth would put it on last of all. Wearing a wig was hot, heavy and uncomfortable, but she would not be seen in public without one. She moved her arms, and frowned still more at the way the skin sagged and flapped. And without her thick make-up, her face looked gaunt, her eyes sunken. Like a death's head, she thought, then pushed the thought away.

She shivered again, more violently. "Mistress Huntly! The window!" she barked. One of the ladies stepped forward to close it. There was noise and clatter in the yard below, and the sound of dogs barking, as if from a sudden arrival.

"What goes on?" demanded the Queen. "What clamour is that? It is full early for a visitor."

Mistress Huntly leaned out, craning her neck. "I cannot tell, Your Majesty. A messenger, perhaps – " but at that moment the double doors of the chamber swung open as if on the breath of a storm. A man burst in, tall, bearded, so bespattered with mud from the road that for a moment he was unrecognisable, even to one who knew him so well. Elizabeth's footmen tried to restrain him, but he batted them away like flies.

"My Lord of Essex!" The Queen rose, aghast. No one was permitted to enter her chamber uninvited. No man was ever allowed to see her in this manner, all disrobed. Why, she had not even time to snatch up her wig! Hot anger burned in her heart, but she kept it concealed.

Essex fell upon his knees. He seized her hand, and pressed kisses upon it. The sight of that noble head, bent low, still moved her. "What is it, my lord, that you have come here to say?"

She listened as Essex protested his loyalty and love, made blustering excuses for his mistakes in Ireland, tried to gloss over any details that might look like treason. Her tone was level, her face a mask. "I hear you, my lord. Now I prithee retire, and when the stains of travel are less evident upon you" – she indicated the splotches of mud on his clothing – "you and I will speak again."

Essex rose, and bowed low. "Your gracious Majesty is merciful. I – "

She dismissed him with a wave of her hand. "I said later, my Lord of Essex." The great doors swung shut behind him. The waiting women stood in a row, holding their breaths. No one dared break the silence.

The Queen gazed into the mirror long and hard, one hand upon her chest as if to still the beating of her aged heart. It was a full quarter-hour before she spoke.

"Mistress Huntly, the emerald silk. Mistress Lane, the slippers of Spanish kid – those with the grass-green lining. Don' t stand there gawping, girl! The day's business must begin."

***

Though Elizabeth stayed calm during Essex's intrusion into her chamber, she knew that he was digging his own grave. He was questioned, and taken into custody. Still she hoped he would reform. The eavesdroppers had reported his treason with Tyrone, but, wanting to give him just one more chance, the Queen didn't tell the Privy Council. He was due to go on trial before the Star Chamber, but he wrote her a humble letter, and she cancelled his trial. She knew she was only playing for time, but, as with Mary, she couldn't bear to condemn someone who mattered to her.

Essex's career was in ruins and he was heavily in debt. He resorted to desperate measures. He told his friends that Elizabeth was "no less crooked and distorted in mind than she was in body". This group of adventurers, Essex's hot-headed friends, met to plan the seizure of the Court, the Tower, and the City of London. Essex wrote to James VI of Scotland for support, hoping to ally himself with Elizabeth's almost certain successor.

Outraged, the Privy Council demanded that Essex report to them. But he refused to go. Two hundred of his followers then rode to the City. Robert Cecil sent a herald denouncing him as a traitor, and an armed force to block the way.

Essex himself was besieged in his house. At last he gave himself up, but only after burning incriminating papers, including letters from James. He was tried in

Westminster Hall, found guilty of treason and condemned to die. Still arrogant, Essex declared, "I owe God a death."

The story goes that Essex had a ring which Elizabeth had once given him, saying that if his life was ever in danger, he should send it to her, and she would rescue him. He entrusted the ring to Lady Nottingham, who deliberately omitted to give it to Elizabeth. Whatever the truth of this story, no pardon was forthcoming. On 25th February 1601, Essex was led out into the courtyard of the Tower of London, and there his head was severed from his body. At the age of thirty-four, the glittering Robert Devereaux, Earl of Essex, was, in his own words, "justly spewed out of the realm."

Elizabeth was beside herself with rage and grief. She knew Essex was a traitor, knew he had to die, but oh, how she missed him! Her godson, Sir John Harington, reported that she had almost stopped eating. "She taketh little but manchet [a white bread roll] and succory potage [soup]... she thrusts her rusty sword into the arras [tapestry] in a great rage." And Elizabeth was not the only one who mourned. Essex was still a popular hero, a celebrity. Ballads were written about his "glorious" life and tragic death. "Sweet England's pride is gone," lamented the balladeers.

Elizabeth, the true pride of "sweet England", was going too. She lived for only two years after Essex's death. She never let old age defeat her; she was a strong and vigorous ruler to the end. She sent Lord Mountjoy to Ireland in place of Essex; he defeated Tyrone, and the Spanish capitulated, so that threat was removed. She acknowledged James VI as her successor, and wrote him letters to prepare him for what lay ahead.

On November 30th, 1601, Elizabeth made a speech to the House of Commons which became known as her "Golden Speech". In it, she summed up her feelings towards the country she had loved and served for so long. "Though God hath raised me high, yet this I account the glory of my crown, that I have reigned with your loves… I never was any greedy, scraping grasper… nor yet a waster; my heart was never set upon any worldly good, but only for my subjects' good… It is not my desire to live or reign longer than my life and reign shall be for your good. And though you have had many mightier and wiser princes sitting in this seat, yet you never had, nor shall have any that will love you better."

On November 17th 1602, Elizabeth celebrated forty-four years on the throne. The following February, she had an audience with an envoy from Venice, who reported on how splendid she looked, decked in silver and white taffeta trimmed with gold, and hung with pearls, rubies and diamonds.

But this splendour was a façade. Her health was failing. She would not take to her bed or see a doctor, but reclined, propped on a pile of cushions. James VI was told on March 19th that Elizabeth could not live three days. He prepared for the journey to London, to claim his throne. Still Elizabeth lingered, taking comfort in the ministrations of Archbishop Whitgift, her "Black Husband", one of the last of her old inner circle. She died, peacefully, between two and three o'clock on the morning of 24th March 1603, "as the most resplendent sun setteth at last in a western cloud."

KEY DATES

25th January 1533 – Anne Boleyn, Elizabeth's mother, marries Henry VIII

7th September 1533 – Elizabeth is born at the royal palace in Greenwich

1547 – Henry VIII dies.

1553 – Elizabeth's half-sister, Mary, becomes queen, after King Edward's death

1559 – After Mary dies, Elizabeth is crowned queen in Westminster Abbey

1559-63 – Parliament introduced the Acts which returned England to the Protestant faith

1568 – Mary, Queen of Scots arrives in England and soon becomes a focus for Catholic plotters

1587 – Mary, Queen of Scots is finally executed

1588 – Phillip II of Spain launches the Spanish Armada, and Elizabeth makes her famous speech to the troops at Tilbury

1603 – Elizabeth dies and is succeeded by the Protestant James VI of Scotland (James I of England), son of Mary Queen of Scots

QUIZ

After you've finished the book, test yourself and see how well you remember what you've read.

1. Henry VIII desperately wanted his wife Anne Boleyn to give birth to:
   Twins
   A daughter
   A son

2. When she was three months old, Elizabeth lived in:
   A house with her own servants
   Her mother's penthouse apartment by the Thames
   Her grandfather's castle in Norfolk

3. Elizabeth's half-sister Mary Tudor was:
   Thin and beautiful
   Short and plain
   Tall and fat

4. For her schooling, her father decided that Elizabeth should:
   Go away to a convent
   Be taught at home by tutors
   Attend the local grammar so she could find out what life was like for ordinary people

5. Elizabeth would spend many hours as a teenager:
   Working out new designs for her bedroom
   Practising her signature
   Trying to get into the pub with her friends

6. Elizabeth and Mary's half-brother Edward became king in 1547 at the age of:
   9
   19
   39

7. When Mary Tudor decided to marry Philip of Spain, the people of England objected by:
   Sending sacks of horse manure to her home
   Throwing snowballs at the Spanish Embassy
   Boycotting Spain as a holiday destination

8. Mary Tudor sent Elizabeth to the Tower of London because:
   Elizabeth didn't invite Mary to her birthday party
   She thought Elizabeth would cheer up the other prisoners
   She believed Elizabeth had been plotting against her

9. Elizabeth's coronation took place on 15 January 1559:
   Because the royal astrologer said it was a lucky day
   To commemorate Henry VIII's birthday
   It was the only date that Westminster Abbey was available

10. Elizabeth gave her close friend Robert Dudley the nickname:
    Mouth
    Toes
    Eyes

11. Elizabeth's cousin Mary Queen of Scots grew up speaking:
    French
    Gaelic
    Romanian

12. The people of England called their much-loved queen Elizabeth I:
    Queenie
    Pollyanna
    Gloriana

13. Elizabethan noblemen loved to wear:
    Stockings, lace and velvet
    Tweed knickerbockers and knitted socks
    Striped tank-tops and combat trousers

14. What was a farthingale?
    A singing street-sweeper
    A stiff frame worn under a skirt
    A coin worth one quarter of a penny

15. Elizabeth's court:
    Ate two vast meals a day
    Made sure they had a balanced diet with five portions
    of fruit and vegetables daily
    Would have take-away venison kebabs sent to the
     palace

16. When Francis Drake returned from his trip round the
world, Elizabeth told him she would:
    Marry him
    Cut off his head
    Make him Master of the Royal Bathtub

17. Elizabeth tried to stop Catholics plotting against her
by:
    Setting up her own secret service
    Destroying the monasteries
    Sending them off to the American colonies

18. Elizabeth rallied her troops at Tilbury before the
Battle of the Armada by:
    Guaranteeing them all a free holiday if they won
    Making a stirring speech
    Promoting everyone two ranks

19. The Earl of Essex, Robert Devereaux, burst into the
Queen's Bedchamber to:
    Congratulate her on her new portrait

Warn her that the Scots were stealing sheep from English farmers

Try and convince Elizabeth that he was her loyal subject

20. Who ruled England after Elizabeth died:

James VI of Scotland

King Eric of Sweden

King Philip of Spain

Charlotte Moore is the author of three novels: *Promises Past*, *Martha's Ark*, and *My Sister,Victoria,*. and one book for children, WHO WAS... Florence Nightingale. Her most recent book was *George And Sam:Autism in the Family*.

Dear Reader,

No matter how old you are, good books always leave you wanting to know more. If you have any questions you would like to ask the author, **Charlotte Moore,** about **Elizabeth I** please write to us at: SHORT BOOKS 15 Highbury Terrace, London N5 1UP.

If you enjoyed this title, then you would probably enjoy others in the series. Why not click on our website for more information and see what the teachers are being told?
www.theshortbookco.com

All the books in the WHO WAS... series are available from TBS, Distribution Centre, Colchester Road, Frating Green, Colchester, Essex CO7 7DW
(Tel: 01206 255800), at £4.99 + P&P.